NUMBAH ONE DAY OF Christmas

written by

Eaton (Bob) Magoon, Jr., Ed Kenney and Gordon N. Phelps

Illustrated by Masaru Yamauchi
edited by Valjeanne Budar

3565 Harding Ave.
Honolulu, Hawai'i 96816
Phone: (800) 910-2377
Fax: (808) 732-3627
www.besspress.com

ISBN 1-1880188-91-0
Library of Congress Catalog Card No: 94-7795

Numbah One day of Christmas, my tutu give to me
One mynah bird in one papaya tree.

Numbah Two day of Christmas, my tutu give to me
Two coconut, an' one mynah bird in one papaya tree.

Numbah Tree day of Christmas, my tutu give to me
Tree dry squid, two coconut,
An' one mynah bird in one papaya tree.

Numbah Foah day of Christmas, my tutu give to me
Foah flowah lei, tree dry squid, two coconut,
An' one mynah bird in one papaya tree.

Numbah Five day of Christmas, my tutu give to me
Five beeg fat peeg . . . foah flowah lei, tree dry squid,
Two coconut, an' one mynah bird in one papaya tree.

Numbah Seex day of Christmas, my tutu give to me
    Seex hula lesson, five beeg fat peeg (that make *ten*!),
    Foah flowah lei, tree dry squid, two coconut,
    An' one mynah bird in one papaya tree.

Numbah Seven day of Christmas, my tutu give to me
Seven shrimp a-swimmin', seex hula lesson,
Five beeg fat peeg, foah flowah lei, tree dry squid,
Two coconut, an' one mynah bird in one papaya tree.

Numbah Eight day of Christmas, my tutu give to me
  Eight ukulele, seven shrimp a-swimmin', seex hula lesson,
  Five beeg fat peeg (that make *twenny*!), foah flowah lei,
  Tree dry squid, two coconut,
  An' one mynah bird in one papaya tree.

Numbah Nine day of Christmas, my tutu give to me
   Nine pound of poi, eight ukulele, seven shrimp a-swimmin',
   Seex hula lesson, five beeg fat peeg, foah flowah lei,
   Tree dry squid, two coconut,
   An' one mynah bird in one papaya tree.

Numbah Ten day of Christmas, my tutu give to me
Ten can of beer, nine pound of poi, eight ukulele,
Seven shrimp a-swimmin', seex hula lesson, five beeg fat peeg,
Foah flowah lei, tree dry squid, two coconut,
An' one mynah bird in one papaya tree.

Numbah Eleven day of Christmas, my tutu give to me
  Eleven missionary, ten can of beer, nine pound of poi,
  Eight ukulele, seven shrimp a-swimmin', seex hula lesson,
  Five beeg fat peeg, foah flowah lei, tree dry squid,
  Two coconut, an' one mynah bird in one papaya tree.

(Numbah Twelve day of Christmas the bes', and the bes' stuff always come las' . . .)

Numbah Twelve day of Christmas, my tutu give to me
  Twelve TELEVISION, eleven missionary, ten can of beer,
  Nine pound of poi, eight ukulele, seven shrimp a-swimmin',
  Seex hula lesson, *forty* steenkin' peeg,
  Foah flowah lei, tree dry squid, two coconut,
  An' one mynah bird in one papaya tree!

NUMBAH ONE DAY OF CHRISTMAS

PIANO-CONDUCTOR

Production

BY EDWARD KENNEY, JR.
GORDON N. PHELPS
EATON MAGOON, JR.

Numbah One day of Christmas, my tutu give to me
One mynah bird in one papaya tree.

Numbah Two day of Christmas, my tutu give to me
Two coconut, an' one mynah bird in one papaya tree.

Numbah Tree day of Christmas, my tutu give to me
Tree dry squid, two coconut,
An' one mynah bird in one papaya tree.

Numbah Foah day of Christmas, my tutu give to me
Foah flowah lei, tree dry squid, two coconut,
An' one mynah bird in one papaya tree.

Numbah Five day of Christmas, my tutu give to me
Five beeg fat peeg . . . foah flowah lei, tree dry squid,
Two coconut, an' one mynah bird in one papaya tree.

Numbah Seex day of Christmas, my tutu give to me
Seex hula lesson, five beeg fat peeg (that make *ten*!),
Foah flowah lei, tree dry squid, two coconut,
An' one mynah bird in one papaya tree.

Numbah Seven day of Christmas, my tutu give to me
Seven shrimp a-swimmin', seex hula lesson,
Five beeg fat peeg, foah flowah lei, tree dry squid,
Two coconut, an' one mynah bird in one papaya tree.

Numbah Eight day of Christmas, my tutu give to me
Eight ukulele, seven shrimp a-swimmin', seex hula lesson,
Five beeg fat peeg (that make *twenny*!), foah flowah lei,
Tree dry squid, two coconut,
An' one mynah bird in one papaya tree.

Numbah Nine day of Christmas, my tutu give to me
Nine pound of poi, eight ukulele, seven shrimp a-swimmin',
Seex hula lesson, five beeg fat peeg, foah flowah lei,
Tree dry squid, two coconut,
An' one mynah bird in one papaya tree.

Numbah Ten day of Christmas, my tutu give to me
Ten can of beer, nine pound of poi, eight ukulele,
Seven shrimp a-swimmin', seex hula lesson, five beeg fat peeg,
Foah flowah lei, tree dry squid, two coconut,
An' one mynah bird in one papaya tree.

Numbah Eleven day of Christmas, my tutu give to me
Eleven missionary, ten can of beer, nine pound of poi,
Eight ukulele, seven shrimp a-swimmin', seex hula lesson,
Five beeg fat peeg, foah flowah lei, tree dry squid,
Two coconut, an' one mynah bird in one papaya tree.

(Numbah Twelve day of Christmas the bes', and the bes' stuff
always come las' . . .)

Numbah Twelve day of Christmas, my tutu give to me
Twelve TELEVISION, eleven missionary, ten can of beer,
Nine pound of poi, eight ukulele, seven shrimp a-swimmin',
Seex hula lesson, *forty* steenkin' peeg,
Foah flowah lei, tree dry squid, two coconut,
An' one mynah bird in one papaya tree!